A New True Book

THE SENECA

By Jill Duvall

CHILDRENS PRESS®

CHICAGO

The Seneca wore wooden false
faces at healing ceremonies.

er, 2, 6 (4 photos), 7, 10,
зу of the Museum of
nois University—DeKalb,

Thomas Gilcrease Institute of American History and
Art, Tulsa, Oklahoma, 33 (cat. #0226)

Historical Pictures Service—9, 25 (right)

© Christine Le Beau—45 (4 photos)

National Museum of American Art/Art Resource,
New York—30

North Wind Picture Archives—4, 13, 20, 21, 25
(left), 28 (3 photos), 37, 39

Photograph Courtesy of Smithsonian Institution
National Museum of the American Indian—11
(neg. #3128), 12 (neg. #1707), 17 (neg. #2635), 19
(neg. #30118), 26 (neg. #37614), 27 (neg. #34852),
43 (left) (neg. #37564), 43 (right) (neg. #1709)

SuperStock International, Inc.—23; © Leonard Lee
Rue, 35

COVER: Iroquois Longhouse
COVER INSET: Seneca Head Mask

Library of Congress Cataloging-in-Publication Data

Duvall, Jill D.
    The Seneca / by Jill D. Duvall.
        p.   cm. — (A New true book)
    Includes index.
    Summary: Examines the history and current situation
of the Seneca Indians.
    ISBN 0-516-01119-7
    1. Seneca Indians—Juvenile literature.
[1. Seneca Indians.   2. Indians of North America.]
I. Title.
E99.S3D88 1991   90-21150
973'.04975—dc20   CIP
                                        AC

NOV 1991

TABLE OF CONTENTS

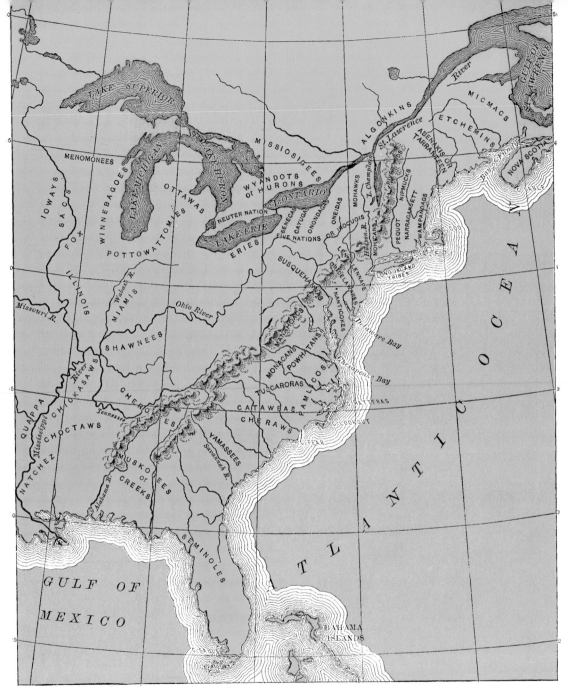

The Seneca lived in the northeastern woodlands of what is now the United States. They called themselves *O-non-dowa-gah*, which means the "Great Hill People." Can you find the Seneca on the map?

THE GREAT HILL PEOPLE

During the ice ages,
glaciers made long, deep
cracks in the earth of New
York State. Clear, icy waters
filled them and created
lakes. One of these was
Lake Canandaigua.

Seneca children are told
that their ancestors emerged
from inside a hill near
Lake Canandaigua and
came onto the earth through
an opening in the hilltop.
That is why the Seneca

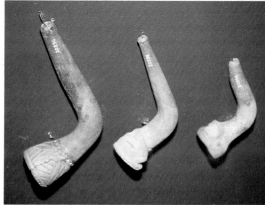

The Seneca made everything from natural materials: Corn-husk funeral moccasins (top left), wooden mask (top right), turtle rattles (above), and clay pipes (right).

called themselves *O-non-dowa-gah*, which means the "Great Hill People."

The Seneca—a mighty warrior nation—belonged to a

The Seneca made many kinds of baskets to carry and store food and other possessions.

group of Native Americans called the Iroquois or Haudenosaunee. They lived in the woodlands in what is now New York State. The Iroquois lived in longhouse villages and farmed small plots of land.

7

THE LONGHOUSE

Longhouses were rectangular buildings that housed several families. The frame was made of small elm tree trunks, or saplings, and covered with bark. The saplings were arched at the top to make the high roof.

Over the door at each end of the building hung the

The longhouse sheltered many families.

totem (emblem) of the
people who lived in the
house—one of the eight
Seneca clans. The members

of a clan were all related
through the female members.
A longhouse might be
from 50 to 200 feet long and
18 to 25 feet wide,
depending on how many
families lived in it.

The families slept on furs spread on the low wooden
platforms at the sides of the longhouse.

A Seneca woman pounds corn with a double-headed wooden mallet. The tub is made from a tree trunk.

VILLAGE LIFE

Seneca men owned their personal possessions, such as clothing and weapons. All other property, including the longhouse and the farming tools, belonged to the women.

11

All the women in a longhouse were sisters, mothers, or daughters of the same family. When a man married, he moved into his wife's longhouse. Seneca children were loved and honored, and elders were respected by the young people.

A Seneca elder woman with a young girl

A Seneca spears fish from an elm-bark canoe.

Senecas traveled in elm-bark canoes, sleds, and toboggans. They fished, hunted, and gathered food from the woods and fields.

The women raised the children and did the farming. They grew corn, beans, and squash.

These Seneca
weapons were
called war clubs.

The men cleared the
fields, fished, hunted, and
taught their sons the ways of
the woods. Warfare and
defense were also jobs for

14 men.

THE FIVE NATIONS

The Iroquois had more warriors than most nations. For a long time, they were involved in constant feuds.

Before the Europeans arrived, however, five of the largest and strongest Iroquois people agreed to stop fighting with one another. The tribes were the Mohawk, Oneida, Onondaga, Cayuga, and Seneca. According to legend, a "peacemaker" brought the plan to them. The five tribes called themselves *Haudenosaunee*, meaning the "People of the Longhouse," because their lands stretched in a line from the Hudson to the Niagara rivers. Their lands reminded them of a longhouse—like several families living under one roof.

The Mohawks, who lived near the Hudson River, were

called Keepers of the
Eastern Door. Seneca
warriors, at the western edge
of the Iroquois territory, were
Keepers of the Western Door.

A boy stands by
the cooking pot in
the "kitchen" area
of a longhouse
built of logs.

17

Wampum was made from beads cut from
purple and white clam shells.

The grand council of the
Haudenosaunee had fifty
chiefs called *sachems*. Two
of these were warrior chiefs.
If talking failed, warrior chiefs
took over from the peace
chiefs. The Seneca warriors
chosen for this honor then
decided if war was to come.

The Iroquois have an oral tradition. Their laws and agreements have passed down through the generations without a written record. They used wampum—beads arranged into special patterns—to help their memories.

Wampum beads were sewn into belts. The patterns of the beads told a story.

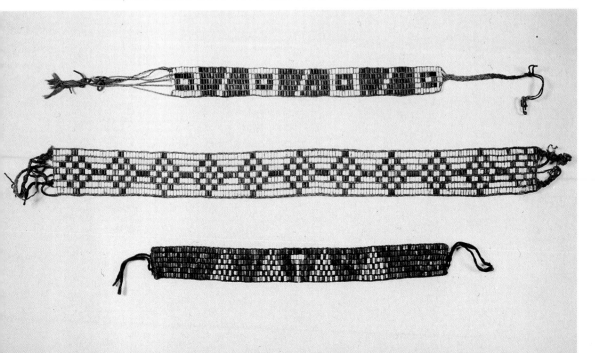

EUROPEANS

The French, who arrived in the area in the 1600s, gave the Five Nations the name *Iroquois*. Father Joseph Chaumonot, a French missionary, was the first European to write about a

Jesuit priests from France came to teach their religion to the Iroquois.

Native Americans traded furs for the manufactured goods of the Europeans.

Seneca village. He counted more than 100 longhouses at Ganondagan in 1656.

The Iroquois taught the French fur traders how to survive in the wilderness. English settlers came next. But the settlers arrived in such large numbers that the Native American life-style was doomed.

THE RIGHT OF DISCOVERY

The claims of the Dutch, French, and English to land in North America caused many wars. The Iroquois of the Five Nations did not believe they could be "owned" by anyone. While they might help one side or another, they always ruled themselves. The Indians did not accept the Europeans' "right of discovery," which meant that explorers could claim their land for monarchs in Europe.

At first, the French and the Seneca were friends. The Indians showed the French fur trappers trails through the dense forest around Niagara Falls. This led to the

On its way from Lake Erie to Lake Ontario, the Niagara River drops over Niagara Falls.

opening of other North American waterways.

But when the French later made an alliance with the Huron people—the most hated of all Seneca enemies—peace was forever shattered between the Seneca and the French. In 1687, the Marquis de Denonville, governor of New France, ordered every Seneca village burned to the ground.

WAR AGAIN

During the American Revolutionary War, many Seneca fought on the British side. In 1779, George Washington, commander of the Continental Army, ordered General John Sullivan to burn all the Seneca villages.

General John Sullivan

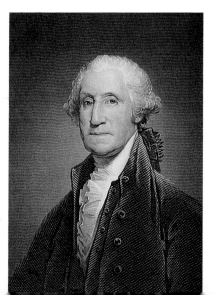

George Washington

A Seneca woman and boy on horseback in the 1800s

Ten years later, Washington
became the first president
of the United States, and
in 1794, President George
Washington made peace

A group of Senecas gather at a log longhouse in the 1800s.

with the Iroquois. The
Cattaraugus and Allegany
reservations in western New
York State were set aside for
the Seneca in the Treaty of
1794.

DEMOCRACY AND THE FIVE NATIONS

Several leaders of the United States were greatly influenced by the democracy of the Haudenosaunee. Benjamin Franklin, Thomas

Benjamin Franklin

James Madison

Thomas Jefferson

Jefferson, and James Madison were among the American statesmen who admired the Five Nations.

Decisions of the Haudenosaunee council had to be agreed upon by every chief. This rule has stood from the founding of the Five Nation confederacy. It is still used today.

George Catlin painted this portrait of a Seneca in the 1800s.

TONAWANDA

In the 1800s, Seneca leaders nearly lost all their lands. The United States government had decided all Native Americans must move west of the Missouri River.

But the Seneca at Tonawanda Reservation in New York State refused to leave. The nation then reached a most creative compromise with the government of the United States. In 1857, the Tonawanda band of Seneca bought back its own land with money that had been set aside by Congress for the move to western lands.

RED JACKET

Chief Sagoyewatha was noted for his inspiring speeches. Even those who didn't understand a word of Seneca could tell he was a great speaker. The name *Sagoyewatha* has been translated as "He who Keeps Them Awake," although "Great Burden Strap" is a better translation of his Seneca name. A jacket given to him by the British earned him his other name— Red Jacket.

George Catlin
painted
Red Jacket
wearing his
silver medal.

In 1792, Red Jacket
received another gift.
President George
Washington presented him
with a beautiful silver medal
representing the friendship
between Red Jacket's people
and the U.S. government.

33

HANDSOME LAKE

Gaiwiio is a Seneca word meaning "the good message." Gaiwiio was brought to the Seneca by a member of their people called Handsome Lake. From 1799 to 1815, Handsome Lake had several visions in which he saw messengers from the Creator of life. These visions were the basis of Gaiwiio, or the longhouse religion, which is now followed by many of the Haudenosaunee.

Gaiwiio has brought a return
to some of the ancient beliefs
that were closely tied to
the land and to nature.

The Native
Americans have
great respect for
nature. They
believe that
humans should
live in harmony
with the land
and with their
animal brothers.

ELY S. PARKER

One well-known Seneca was Ely S. Parker. Hasanoanda was Parker's Seneca name. When Ely S. Parker was a young Seneca in Tonawanda, he learned English and met an American named Lewis Henry Morgan. In 1851, Ely S. Parker became a sachem of the Haudenosaunee council. That same year, Morgan

Ely S. Parker's
Seneca name
was Hasanoanda.

published a book about the
native culture of the
Iroquois people.

Parker became a general
in the Union Army during the
Civil War. Parker's skill as a
diplomat was well known. In

fact, it was Ely Parker who wrote out the terms of surrender for General Robert E. Lee to sign at Appomattox Court House on April 9, 1865. The Civil War soon ended.

General Parker was then Ulysses S. Grant's military secretary. More important, he was his friend.

Ely S. Parker (at table at right) was at Appomattox Court House when General Robert E. Lee signed the surrender papers.

Later, as president of the United States, Grant appointed General Parker Commissioner of Indian Affairs. Parker was the first Seneca and Native American to serve in that office.

Senecas stand beside a totem pole carved
by a man from the Cattaraugus Reservation.

THE RESERVATIONS

The Cattaraugus and
Allegany reservations are
still owned by the Seneca
people, now called the
Seneca Nation of Indians.

In 1843, the Seneca Nation adopted a written constitution. Today their government is made up of a council of sixteen members, elected every two years. Eight members come from each reservation.

The Seneca on the Tonawanda Reservation have a different government. They are ruled by their chiefs.

In the 1800s, railroad companies began asking for

rights-of-way through the Seneca Nation territory in western New York. When those rights were granted, non-Indians began settling on the reservation land along the railroads.

For many years there have been problems with towns that were settled in this way. According to the Treaty of 1794, Congress had to approve all land arrangements on Indian reservations in order to protect the Indians from land grabbers. Leases were

A new-style longhouse (left) on the Cattaraugus Reservation. William Blueskye, a Seneca, lived on the Cattaraugus Reservation.

required, and non-Indian settlers were asked to pay rent. Although the rents were very low, many settlers didn't pay them. This situation has continued for more than ninety-nine years.

Land claims are now reaching the highest courts.

Several decisions have recently returned lands to their original owners—the Iroquois nations.

Some of the land problems were addressed when President George Bush signed the Seneca Nation Resettlement Act of 1990. The Seneca will receive some money for the rents due them from land leases. The city of Salamanca, New York, will be allowed to renew its lease.

Seneca children try to keep their traditional values
while preparing for the future in the modern world.

The Haudenosaunee people
have remained strong. They
have kept their traditions
and beliefs alive not only
for the children of today
but also for the children of
many generations to come.

WORDS YOU SHOULD KNOW

ancestor (AN • sess • ter) — a grandparent or forebear earlier in history

clan (KLAN) — a group of related families descended from a common ancestor

compromise (KAHM • pruh • myz) — a settlement of a dispute in which each side gives up some of what it wants

confederacy (kun • FED • er • ih • see) — a union or league of states or groups of people for a common purpose

constitution (KAHN • stih • too • shun) — a system of basic laws or rules for a government

council (KOWN • sill) — a group of people meeting to discuss plans or to give advice

diplomat (DIP • luh • mat) — a person who carries on relations between different nations or groups of people

explorer (ex • PLOR • er) — a person who travels to an unknown part of the world to find out more about it

feud (FYOOD) — a fight; a conflict

generation (jen • er • AY • shun) — all the individuals born at about the same time; parents are one generation and children are the next

glacier (GLAY • sher) — a large, riverlike field of ice

Haudenosaunee (how • den • uh • SAW • nee) — an Iroquois word meaning "People of the Longhouse"

Iroquois (EAR • ih • kwoy) — the French name for the tribes of the Five Nations; the Haudenosaunee

longhouse (LAWNG • howss) — a long, narrow dwelling built of poles set in the ground and arched at the top, then covered with sheets of bark

missionary (MISH • uh • nair • ee) — a person who travels to another country to bring a certain religion to the people there

monarch (MAHN • ark) — a king or queen; sole ruler

rectangular (rek • TANG • yoo • ler) — shaped like a figure that has four right angles and four sides

renew (rih • NOO) — to make new again; to start again

reservation (reh • zer • VAY • shun) — a piece of land set aside by the government as a home for an Indian tribe

right-of-way (RITE • uv • way) — a strip of land set aside for a railroad to build track through a region

sachem (SAYCH • im) — a chief

sapling (SAP • ling) — a small, slender young tree

territory (TAIR • ih • tor • ee) — an area of land that a group of people regard as their own

toboggan (tuh • BAH • ghin) — a long flat sled without runners, curved upward at the front

totem (TOH • tum) — an object, such as an animal, serving as a symbol for a family or clan

tribe (TRYB) — a group of people related by blood and customs

vision (VIZJ • un) — something seen in the mind, as in a dream

wampum (WAHM • pum) — small beads made of shells and sewn into patterns on belts, etc.; used by the Indians as money, and to record events

warrior (WOR • ee • er) — a person trained for fighting; a soldier

INDEX

About the Author

Jill Duvall is a political scientist who received an M.A. from Georgetown University in 1976. Since then, her research and writing have included a variety of national and international issues. Among these are world hunger, alternative energy, human rights, cross-cultural and interracial relationships. One of her current endeavors is a study of ancient goddess cultures. Ms. Duvall proudly serves as a member of the Board of Managers of the Glen Mills Schools, a facility that is revolutionizing methods for rehabilitating male juvenile delinquents.